The leek. A poem on St David's day. Most humbly inscrib'd to the honourable society of Antient Britons, establish'd in honour of Her Royal Highness's birth-day, and the principality of Wales. By N. Griffith, Esq.

N. Griffith

The leek. A poem on St David's day. Most humbly inscrib'd to the honourable society of Antient Britons, establish'd in honour of Her Royal Highness's birth-day, and the principality of Wales. By N. Griffith, Esq.
Griffith, N. (Nehemiah)
ESTCID: T103006
Reproduction from British Library

London : printed by W. Wilkins, for W. Hinchliffe, 1717.
[2],29,[1]p. ; 2°

Eighteenth Century
Collections Online
Print Editions

Gale ECCO Print Editions

Relive history with *Eighteenth Century Collections Online*, now available in print for the independent historian and collector. This series includes the most significant English-language and foreign-language works printed in Great Britain during the eighteenth century, and is organized in seven different subject areas including literature and language; medicine, science, and technology; and religion and philosophy. The collection also includes thousands of important works from the Americas.

The eighteenth century has been called "The Age of Enlightenment." It was a period of rapid advance in print culture and publishing, in world exploration, and in the rapid growth of science and technology – all of which had a profound impact on the political and cultural landscape. At the end of the century the American Revolution, French Revolution and Industrial Revolution, perhaps three of the most significant events in modern history, set in motion developments that eventually dominated world political, economic, and social life.

In a groundbreaking effort, Gale initiated a revolution of its own: digitization of epic proportions to preserve these invaluable works in the largest online archive of its kind. Contributions from major world libraries constitute over 175,000 original printed works. Scanned images of the actual pages, rather than transcriptions, recreate the works *as they first appeared.*

Now for the first time, these high-quality digital scans of original works are available via print-on-demand, making them readily accessible to libraries, students, independent scholars, and readers of all ages.

For our initial release we have created seven robust collections to form one the world's most comprehensive catalogs of 18th century works.

Initial Gale ECCO Print Editions collections include:

History and Geography
Rich in titles on English life and social history, this collection spans the world as it was known to eighteenth-century historians and explorers. Titles include a wealth of travel accounts and diaries, histories of nations from throughout the world, and maps and charts of a world that was still being discovered. Students of the War of American Independence will find fascinating accounts from the British side of conflict.

Social Science
Delve into what it was like to live during the eighteenth century by reading the first-hand accounts of everyday people, including city dwellers and farmers, businessmen and bankers, artisans and merchants, artists and their patrons, politicians and their constituents. Original texts make the American, French, and Industrial revolutions vividly contemporary.

Medicine, Science and Technology
Medical theory and practice of the 1700s developed rapidly, as is evidenced by the extensive collection, which includes descriptions of diseases, their conditions, and treatments. Books on science and technology, agriculture, military technology, natural philosophy, even cookbooks, are all contained here.

Literature and Language
Western literary study flows out of eighteenth-century works by Alexander Pope, Daniel Defoe, Henry Fielding, Frances Burney, Denis Diderot, Johann Gottfried Herder, Johann Wolfgang von Goethe, and others. Experience the birth of the modern novel, or compare the development of language using dictionaries and grammar discourses.

Religion and Philosophy
The Age of Enlightenment profoundly enriched religious and philosophical understanding and continues to influence present-day thinking. Works collected here include masterpieces by David Hume, Immanuel Kant, and Jean-Jacques Rousseau, as well as religious sermons and moral debates on the issues of the day, such as the slave trade. The Age of Reason saw conflict between Protestantism and Catholicism transformed into one between faith and logic -- a debate that continues in the twenty-first century.

Law and Reference
This collection reveals the history of English common law and Empire law in a vastly changing world of British expansion. Dominating the legal field is the *Commentaries of the Law of England* by Sir William Blackstone, which first appeared in 1765. Reference works such as almanacs and catalogues continue to educate us by revealing the day-to-day workings of society.

Fine Arts
The eighteenth-century fascination with Greek and Roman antiquity followed the systematic excavation of the ruins at Pompeii and Herculaneum in southern Italy; and after 1750 a neoclassical style dominated all artistic fields. The titles here trace developments in mostly English-language works on painting, sculpture, architecture, music, theater, and other disciplines. Instructional works on musical instruments, catalogs of art objects, comic operas, and more are also included.

The BiblioLife Network

This project was made possible in part by the BiblioLife Network (BLN), a project aimed at addressing some of the huge challenges facing book preservationists around the world. The BLN includes libraries, library networks, archives, subject matter experts, online communities and library service providers. We believe every book ever published should be available as a high-quality print reproduction; printed on-demand anywhere in the world. This insures the ongoing accessibility of the content and helps generate sustainable revenue for the libraries and organizations that work to preserve these important materials.

The following book is in the "public domain" and represents an authentic reproduction of the text as printed by the original publisher. While we have attempted to accurately maintain the integrity of the original work, there are sometimes problems with the original work or the micro-film from which the books were digitized. This can result in minor errors in reproduction. Possible imperfections include missing and blurred pages, poor pictures, markings and other reproduction issues beyond our control. Because this work is culturally important, we have made it available as part of our commitment to protecting, preserving, and promoting the world's literature.

GUIDE TO FOLD-OUTS MAPS and OVERSIZED IMAGES

The book you are reading was digitized from microfilm captured over the past thirty to forty years. Years after the creation of the original microfilm, the book was converted to digital files and made available in an online database.

In an online database, page images do not need to conform to the size restrictions found in a printed book. When converting these images back into a printed bound book, the page sizes are standardized in ways that maintain the detail of the original. For large images, such as fold-out maps, the original page image is split into two or more pages

Guidelines used to determine how to split the page image follows:

• Some images are split vertically; large images require vertical and horizontal splits.
• For horizontal splits, the content is split left to right.
• For vertical splits, the content is split from top to bottom.
• For both vertical and horizontal splits, the image is processed from top left to bottom right.

THE LEEK.

A POEM

ON St DAVID's DAY.

Most Humbly Inscrib'd to the Honourable
SOCIETY of *ANTIENT BRITONS*,
Establish'd in Honour of Her ROYAL HIGHNESS'S
Birth-Day, and the Principality of WALES.

By *N. GRIFFITH*, Esq;

Pan so sôn am Ddigoniant,
Dy roi'n vwch pob Dewr a wnant!   *Tudur Penllyn.*

LONDON:
Printed by W. WILKINS, for W. HINCHLIFFE, at *Dryden's*
Head under the *Royal-Exchange*. MDCCXVII.

THE
LEEK.

HAIL to the Day, that crown'd with DAVID's Name,
Stands confecrated to eternal Fame;
Thy glad Solemnities his Worth shall speak,
That foil'd the *Saxons*, and obtain'd the LEEK:
While in our glowing Breasts the Patriot's Praise
Shall warm Incentives to new Honours raise.

So, sacred *Bards* of old, in Layes inspir'd,
The Youth to noble Emulation fir'd,
High Deeds of Ancestors to view they plac'd,
And urg'd to future Glory from the past.

O BRITONS! could the Muse give Rage so strong,
And furnish Numbers equal to the Song;
Your own AUGUSTUS should not daunt her Flight,
Nor LONGUEVILLE hear unpleas'd what she'd recite.

NOW had *Britannia* long endur'd the Weight,
Of all the Woes that press a sinking State:
Hard Fortune bore; but yet saw worse behind,
And Foes still rising as her Strength declin'd.
The *Saxons* then, a People fam'd afar,
Well disciplin'd to Government and War,
(Their Fleets o'er spacious Fields of Ocean spread,
And mighty *Woden*'s Sons their Armies led)
Bend their whole Force to seize the wasted *Isle*,
Yet no cheap Conquest found, nor bloodless Toil.
But many a brave tho' fruitless Struggle past,
The *Britons* only cou'd retreat at last.

Then DAVID rose, a venerable Seer,
In Sanctity of Life without a Peer,
By Heaven ordain'd fresh Ardor to infuse,
And in these Words their Courage he renews.

And is it thus, our Country we defend?
Must then the *British* Name inglorious end?
Not so our Fathers shun'd the fatal Field,
Or to the Conqu'rors of the World did yield:
Not so these very *Saxons* e'er cou'd boast
The smallest Share of our dear Country lost:
Is it for Love of Life, we're Cowards grown?
Oh, what is Life when *Liberty* is gone!
Can we live Slaves beneath the Victor's Hand?
Or Fugitives in our own Native Land?

Stung with the just Reproach, they all declare
Once more to try the nobler Fate of War;
Each Bosom burns with the old generous Flame,
And for the Fight they now a Leader claim:
Fall'n in the War are all our Chiefs, they said,
And who but DAVID can our Armies head?
Thy self of our once glorious Royal Line,
Nor does thy Virtue from thy Birth decline!
They bravely for our Country gave their Breath,
And thou shalt lead to *Liberty* or *Death*.

Then strait dispers'd, nor his Reply attend,
And quick th' Alarm thro' their whole Nation send:
All catch the Word; and studious of the War,
The Instruments of Battel now prepare;
To the bright Sword its keenest Edge impart,
New string the tough Yeugh Bow, and point the Dart.
Ev'n hoary Age rekindling Vigour warms,
And beardless Youth essay the Weight of Arms.

Mean while the Pious Chief, with anxious Thought,
Menevia's solitary Desart sought.
A Land forlorn and waste; the steril Ground
Did with bare Stones, a hopeless Crop! abound:
Nor here the yellow Harvest e'er was seen,
Nor Pasture cloath'd the Soil with chearful Green;
No rising Woods the naked Surface hide,
Nor winding Streams the joyless Glebe divide;

On

On the bleak Coast the gath'ring Tempests swell,
And only whistling Winds for ever dwell.

Seven Times his radiant Course the circling Sun
Along the Azure Plains of Heav'n had run;
As oft the Moon advanc'd with borrow'd Light,
To chear the gloomy Season of the Night:
While here alone the tedious Term he pass'd,
In heavy dumb Affliction; till at last
With gushing Tears he gave his Griefs a Vent,
And loudly did his Country's Fate lament:
Prostrate on Earth his Pray'r to Heav'n address'd,
And thus the Anguish of his Soul express'd.

O POWER SUPREME! whose everlasting Sway
Nature and all her varying Turns obey;
Nor varying are to Thee; but constant still,
The meer Effects of thy own Sov'reign Will!
Thy wide Dominion spreads to ev'ry Land,
And Empires rise and fall at thy Command.
Gracious, thy *Britain* now behold! e'er while
Thy chosen Nation, and thy favour'd *Isle!*
With thy indulgent Blessing amply crown'd,
Peace undisturb'd and Plenty smil'd around,
That other Lands were happy, as they shar'd
Of what our overflowing Fulness spar'd.
But more, e'en Heaven it self descended here,
And *Gospel* yet but dawning did appear;

Here

Here *first* did in the Regal Purple shine,
And sav'd a *Lucius* and a *Constantine*:
And from the vast Success it here obtain'd,
Assent from Nations unbelieving gain'd!
Why then such Miracles of Goodness shewn,
Dost thou in Anger now reject thy own?

But ah, the Cause too easy to unfold!
Oh Shame! Oh Grief! Oh Horror to be told!
Our Guilt! ---- How fatally our Guilt conspires
To justify the worst thy Wrath requires!
And who, ah who, from the Infection free?
What Age, or Sex, Profession, or Degree?
Our Princes grasp at dire unbounded Pow'r,
Not to protect and govern, but devour:
Faith, Law, nor Reason, circumscribe their Sway,
And none are Subjects who are not their Prey!
Judges, Partiality and Bribes pervert,
Nor longer they will Equity assert:
The Prisoners sigh, th' Oppress'd appeal to Thee,
For none will hear on Earth to set them free!
Ev'n we, thy Prophets, greater yet the Shame!
Prophets (nor worthy that) alone in Name!
Ev'n we, as if to pull thy Vengeance down,
The common Guilt too weak, add all our own:
In th' empty Title, much, too much, we pride,
But all the painful Duties lay aside:

No longer now is *Peace on Earth* our Care,
Good-Will to Men no longer we declare:
We a new Function to our selves create,
To raise Dissentions and embroil our State:
Habitual Sloth still deadens what we preach,
And Luxury is all we practically teach!
No wonder our abandon'd Flocks transgress,
When we their Pastors sin to such Excess!
Corruption of our Manners loudly cries
Defiance to, or Vengeance from, the Skies:
How then can Justice hold its lifted Hand?
Nor thou avenge thy self on such a Land!
Ah! hence, 'tis hence thy angry Judgments flow!
And this the fatal Source of all our Woe!
This brought the *Pagan Saxons* to our *Isle*:
This gives us to the Sword, and to the Spoil,
This does in Dust our Habitations lay;
And ev'n thy Temples mix with common Clay!

 Yet Guilty as we are; with Pity see,
Distress'd we humbly bow our selves to thee!
Righteous we own the Judgments thou hast sent;
Confess and loath our Vileness, and repent.
For thou, (and thine alone it is to do)
Can'st give Repentance, and Remission too!
O yet return - our low Estate behold,
Record thy Loving-kindnesses of Old!

Again thy long absented Succour lend,
Nor make a full irrevocable End.

Ev'n now in vain we arm against the Foe,
Unless thou forth wilt with our Armies go:
We else but meet our Fate, and hasten down
Fell Ruin, on a People once thine own!
Vengeance, 'tis true, thy *Justice* may demand
But cannot *Mercy* spare a guilty Land?

He spoke, and soon were all his Sorrows lost,
And holy Transports his whole Soul engross'd:
Comforts Divine profusely on him flow'd,
Scarce could Mortality sustain the Load.
Grateful he took the Proof of Heav'ns Regard,
Nor fail'd in Praises that his Pray'r was heard.

He feels new Springs of lively Vigor beat,
And now inspired with more than Martial Heat,
Direct to *Isca* takes his way, for there
The *Britons* had appointed to repair.
Isca then was: *Isca* an ancient Town,
For splendid State, and goodly Structure known
On Walls of Brick, *Rome*'s nicest Art, were found
The lofty Ramparts that her Circuit bound.
'Twas long e'er envious Time could quite erase
All Tracks of Pristine Grandeur from the Place:
Here stop'd the gazing Trav'ller to behold
Heaps, that were spacious Palaces of old;

Th

That once advanc'd in all the *Roman* Pride,
Far by their gilded Pinacles defcry'd.
The famous Tow'r of huge Gigantick Size,
That feem'd afpiring to invade the Skies;
And Baths, that fuch Magnificence did boaft,
Now in the dark promifcuous Rubbifh loft.
Here the three Temples that of old had been,
Were only in their awful Ruins feen:
And there a Length of Wall, ftill nodding, told,
It once did Circques and Theaters infold.
Nor only thefe, but ev'n within the Ground
Were fubterranean Edifices found:
There Aquæducts with wonder ftrike the Eyes,
And curious vaulted Paffages furprife;
And Lamps conceal'd (ftupendious Pow'r of Art!)
Did, like the Sun above, due Warmth impart.
The whole the utmoft Force of Skill exprefs'd,
And well its *Roman* Origin confefs'd.

From the brave Legions here *Caerlheon* came;
In after Ages *Ifca*'s other Name.

Here too the Patriarchs fix'd their pompous Seat,
Till DAVID chofe *Menevia*'s poor Retreat:
His poor *Menevia*, more for Heaven inclin'd,
Which fuited beft his *Poverty of Mind*.

On *Oske*'s fair Banks the noble City ftood,
And fent her loaded Gallies down the Flood.

Tall Hills aloof defend againſt the Storm,
And ſhady Groves the beauteous Landſkip form:
The riſing Town o'erlook'd the Chryſtal Tide,
And Meadows ſpread beneath their verdant Pride.

Here from all Parts the *Britons* form their Way,
And forward ſpring to the important Day.
Succeſſive Shouts along the Air rebound,
And the ſhrill Trumpets mix their brazen Sound.
Each Band beneath their proper Chiefs advance,
Who at their Head on neighing Courſers praunce.

The ſtout *Silures* firſt the Battel fought,
Them to the Field their great *Tredegar* brought.
In him the true old *Briton* beſt was ſeen,
The generous Soul ſincere, and artleſs Mien:
Not large Poſſeſſions could elate his Mind,
But ſtill he knew himſelf of Human Kind:
He ne'er the Pomp of ſwelling Titles priz'd,
But ſaw through the thin Outſide, and deſpis'd;
In vain they his plain honeſt Heart would move,
There, the ſole Paſſion was his Country's Love!
Such Glory does *Tredegar*'s Name afford!
And his *Silures* worthy ſuch a Lord!
They, a couragious Race, inur'd to War,
Untaught the Yoke of Servitude to bear;
A ſtubborn People them the *Romans* ſtile,
Whom Force could not ſubdue, nor Fraud beguile.

When *Claudius* raging, their Destruction swore,
And proudly said, their Name should be no more;
Their noble Souls exasperated grew,
With Indignation, strait to Arms they flew:
'Twas he, the bold *Caradoc!* led them on,
Nor sure a braver *Briton* e'er was known:
Not brutal Rashness in his Bosom glow'd,
Nor vulgar Courage his Atchievements shew'd;
Sedate amidst a Thousand Deaths he stands,
Nor less himself than the whole Host commands:
His high Attempts right Conduct ever crown'd,
Nor great *Cassibelan* was so renown'd.
Ev'n in Disgrace, (so Providence ordains!)
Still the same Greatness of his Soul remains:
Th' illustrious Captive from his native Home
They bore, in Triumph to expose at *Rome*;
Not so his Dignity of Carriage claim'd;
Ev'n *Claudius* to Humanity was sham'd!

 Next, the Co-partners of *Siluria*'s Fame
Into the Camp the rough *Dimetæ* came.

 Audoen leads from *Penbro*'s fertile Ground,
And Coasts where Fish and foreign Wines abound,
Where Winds, across the streighten'd Ocean, bear
Salubrious Breezes of *Hibernian* Air.

 In shining Equipage, *Vauganus* went
Before the Troops *Ceretica* had sent;

From tow'ring Hills, and flow descending Plains,
That hold the sparkling Oar in silver Veins;
And from the *Champain* Lands, along the Coast
On which the loud *Vergivian* Waves are toss'd.

 Caerwynter does his *Marıdunians* head,
From the fair Region that old *Merdhin* bred,
The *Britons* ever to his Lore attend,
And but with Time it self his Predicts end.

 The *Ordovices Celemundel* brought,
They for the native Freedom longest fought:
A Race, whom fierce impetuous Ardor warms,
And ever ravish'd with the Clank of Arms!

 From the *Valdwinan* Country they proceed,
Renown'd for Horses of the choicest Breed:
From *Mediolanum* their glad Way they take,
And hasty Marches from *Maglona* make.

 From the *Mervinian* Mountains they descend,
That ragged Tops among the Clouds protend;
So thick together, too their Heights they rear,
They hang almost contiguous in the Air,
That oft the Shepherds, as their Flocks they guide,
Hold Talk from bellying Rocks on either side:
But if in homely Taunts they once engage,
And kindle up their angry Souls to Rage;
Scarce the whole Length of Summer Days allows
The Clowns to meet beneath and fall to Blows.

          From

From the dark Isle, the *Druids* ancient Seat,
(Who in thick Woods did myſtick Rites repeat)
Mona, that with her Wheat all *Cambria* fed,
They march along with *Merig* at their Head.

From old *Segontium*, and the *Gangan* Shore,
Where the *Hibernian* Ocean's Billows roar,
Ruffinus led, who did his Lineage trace
From the great Princes of the *Britiſh* Race.
From the ſublime *Arvonian* Alps they go,
Whoſe Heads are white with everlaſting Snow:
They follow *Gedior* from *Eryri*'s Sides,
And from the Vallies where *Conovius* glides.

They come that on the *Denbian* Confines dwell,
Where high the bare unfruitful Mountains ſwell:
Yet there, to ſhew how Nature can command,
She ſpreads the faireſt Vale in *Britiſh* Land;
There the gay Pomp of Woods and Meads appears,
And *Cluyd* along in wanton Mazes errs:
They with *Robartas* leave the pregnant Soil,
And *Salbur* ſummons to a nobler Toil,
Nor more the Joys of blooming Life have Charms,
His *Country* calls the gallant Youth to Arms!

From Lands, where *Roman Varus* left his Name,
And *Elwy*'s Banks with *Dawides* they came:
From the rich Hills, where Minerals are found,
And Fields with bending Harveſt early crown'd:

There

There *Alen*'s Streams beneath the Mountain flow,
And run unseen their silent Course below;
E'er long they burst again to open Day,
And through the Dales in loose Meanders stray.

They come, in distant *Melor* that reside,
And they, that drink of *Deva*'s holy Tide.

Selected out of all, the chosen Band
Fell to the brave *Cadwgawn* to command:
In graceful Aspect he excell'd, and best
In his bold Look the Soldier stood confess'd.
Him DAVID did with glad Surprise behold,
And thus his inward Joy the Prophet told.

O *Briton*! now we see Heaven's kind Intent,
And thou the Angel of Deliv'rance sent:
O welcome to the Camp! nor only share,
But thine be all the Honours of the War!
Thee a long Train of Victories await;
Haste, O Restorer of *Britania*'s State!
Full well, nor is the Omen vain! I see
The old *Caradoc* live again in thee:
Be it thy Task his Footsteps to pursue,
And keep the glorious Pattern still in view:
In thee may his bright Conduct ever shine,
And oh, may his propitious God be thine!

Mean time; the Enemy no less prepare,
And all their Pow'rs assembled for the War.

Conquest thus far attends our Arms, they said,
And shall we now a vanquish'd People dread?
Long since our warlike Sires expell'd the Race;
And left us but the Fugitives to chase.

With such insulting Boasts the *Saxons* arm,
And to the Field in untold Numbers swarm.

When now they had the *British* Camp in sight,
They call a Council to ordain the Fight:
There soon the easy Measures were agreed,
And forth they gave the Signal to proceed.
Then impious *Fosto* a loud Outcry made,
And thus with vain Harangue their March delay'd.

Saxons! ah, whither haste we thus away,
When now the Sun has measur'd half the Day!
Believe me, (once alas! a *Briton* too)
The Work is not to fight, but to pursue:
Think you so vast a Toil is thus sustain'd,
And only, like the Battel, quickly gain'd?
Or do you in Compassion wish, that Night
May cover the vile Wretches in their Flight?
Else sure, with early Day should be begun,
A Chase not finish'd with the setting Sun!
Mark my Advice then, and no less propose
Than now at once to crush our hated Foes:
Urge to its last Advantage the Defeat,
And all your Victories in this compleat!

" ... perchance, while hot Pursuit we make,
We should each other for the Foe mistake,
Let us assume some fit Distinction all,
To shew the raging *Seax* where not to fall!

He ceas'd: In Shouts they give their glad Assent,
And the whole Air with Acclamations rent.
They halt, and into Line of Battel drawn,
Expect impatient the next Morning's Dawn.
Nor wanted the Distinction; near they found
A fertile Field with rising Verdure crown'd:
They pluck the beauteous Plants, whose Blades ascend,
And their green Length from silver Roots extend,
Then on their Head-Plates, with too timely haste,
The happy Sign triumphantly they plac'd.

Rang'd in the Front, a base perfidious Brood
Of odious Renegado *Britons* stood:
Them *Foslo* marshal'd on the guilty Plain;
And faithless *Gurmund* with his *Irish* Train.
Him thence the *Britons* did invite at first
To aid against their Foes, himself the worst!
His lawless Tribe wide Devastations make,
But most on sacred Piles their Fury wreak.

The *Saxon* Kings each his own Subjects led,
And all acknowledg'd *Cymric* for their Head.
The potent Monarch, whose superior Sway
Princes of other Provinces obey!

The Chief did the *Weſtſeaxnan* Scepter wield,
And brought a thouſand Squadrons to the Field.

O'er the *Suthſeaxas Aiſkwin* did preſide,
Who loud the *Britons*, and their God, defy'd:
Aloft he ſhook his Spear, by *Woden*, *Thor*,
And all his Gods, the mad Blaſphemer ſwore!

Ermenric, who from *Hengiſt* claim'd Deſcent,
March'd fiercely from the fatal Shores of *Kent*:
There firſt the *Romans* trod on *Britiſh* Ground,
And there the *Saxons* their firſt Entry found,
In three ſmall Barks and under the Command
Of *Hengiſt*, and of *Huſa*, came to Land.

O *Vortigern*! may thy deteſted Name
Be ſtill deliver'd down to endleſs Shame!
Thou Traitor, who for a curs'd *Saxon* Maid,
Thy Crown, thy Country, and thy Faith betray'd!

Next valiant *Saithelm*, the *Eaſtſeaxnan* King,
Did to the Field his ſturdy Vaſſals bring.

And Lords unnumber'd of inferior Name,
From all the Lands as far as *Tweſis* came

And now the ruddy Morn ſprang forth to Sight,
Streaking the Eaſtern Skies with bluſhing Light.
The ſprightly Trumpets tell th' Approach of Day,
And the rouz'd Horſes for the Battel neigh.
Loud Shouts from either Hoſt like Rage declare,
And clatt'ring Arms reſound the Din of War.

So two fierce Lions on the *Lybian* Plain
Roar from afar, and shake their brinded Manes
From fervid Nostrils Clouds of Smoke they breathe,
And spurn with griping Paws the Sand beneath

Before his *Britons* their great Leader stood,
With careful Eye the whole Batalion view'd:
Then stretch'd his Arm, at which from either End
They close their Ranks, and half around him bend.
When lo! with dread Amazement they perceive
The solid Ground with quick Convulsions heave,
Till by degrees the Earth officious rears,
And high a Throne of grassy Turf appears!
The Miracle, to Joy their first Surprize
Soon chang'd, and Peals of Praise ascend the Skies:
The while, to sight unmov'd, the Godlike Man
Commanding Silence mounts, and thus began:

Once more, O *Britons!* thus in Arms we stand,
T' attempt the Rescue of our Native Land
Our glorious Fathers oft in Battel try'd,
What this Great Day for ever must decide:
This the important Crisis of our Fate,
Compleats our Slav'ry, or restores our State!
The Treach'rous *Saxons* now, with lawless Might,
Pretending Title, have usurp'd our Right
But how their Claim commenc'd, your selves may see.
Or briefly sum'd, receive it thus from me.

F.

Long had gay Halcyon Days on *Britain* shore,
To *Rome*'s politer Arts and Manners won:
Nor could her *Cæsars*, when they gain'd our Coast,
Throughout their World so fair a Province boast:
Hence the fierce Soldier did the Cohort grace,
And hence *Ruffina's* beautify'd their Race
But Empire has its Date, nor could ev'n *Rome*
Assert Exemption from impending Doom.
Her Councils sage, and Arms victorious, fail!
Nor all the Pow'r of *Britain* drain'd avail!
Sole Monarchy, and wide Extent of Sway,
To its own Ruin does it self betray:
Far distant Realms at once distract her Reign,
(Invaded or revolted) to retain
Nor wanted civil Feud, and mad Debate,
The certain Prelude to a falling State!

With *Rome* fell *Britain*, and abandon'd lay
To ev'ry rude Invader now a Prey.
In vain she now would back require her Sons,
And to loose Air she gives her fruitless Groans!

The *Picts*, a savage Race from Men expell'd,
The *Caledonian* Wilds and Forrests held:
In Routs along the Waste they howl for Food,
Or fream in Sounders through the trembling Wood.
Them Time to come the *Highland-Clans* shall name;
In all but Appellation still the same:

But

But oh! shall ever *Britons* join the War
Or languish for such Ravishers the Fair!
These leave their Haunts, with Lust and Rapine foam,
And in dire Havock o'er *Britania* roam.
Nought but Maids Shrieks, and Infants Cries are heard,
And Fire and Sword through all the Region glar'd.
Ev'n Flight would here have fail'd its poor Redress,
And only but have doubled the Distress
The heaving Waves gape hollow Death before,
And Rage behind and horrid Slaughter roar,
On either Hand a wretched Choice is found,
Or to be Butcher'd there, or here be Drown'd!

 Yet was not *Britain* doom'd (if doom'd at all)
By these, but nobler Hands at least, to fall.

 For then, or Chance, or Destiny, brought o'er
A Crew of wandring *Saxons* to our Shore:
In right good Time the welcome Guests propose
To join their Arms, against our barb'rous Foes;
And if too weak the Aid they could impart,
Their whole brave Nation should our Rights assert!
Then soon the urgent Message was dispatch'd,
Which no less eagerly the *Saxons* catch'd:
Pouring from their own Lands whole Droves arrive,
Nor fail the Villain *Picts* away to drive.
But then, alas! behind new Ruin lies,
What Foes more dang'rous than too strong Allies?

Inhospitable Arms on us they bend,
And seize what they were sent for to defend:
Worse than the very *Picts*; outrageous grown,
They challenge now our Kingdoms for their own!
Our Fathers long their Violence withstood,
And seal'd their Country's Love with dying Blood!
But see! now here they come! These, these are they,
That claim our Country and our Lives their Prey!
Bear bravely on to Vict'ry and Applause!
Britons the Men! and *Liberty* the Cause!

Britons and *Liberty*! aloud they cry,
In Shouts as loud the *Saxon* Host reply:
Then strait from twanging Bows the Arrows sent,
On Death's first distant Errands swiftly went;
The feather'd Storms pour thick from either Side,
And in dark Clouds the whole Horizon hide.

So each collected Show'r of harden'd Rain
Comes patt'ring all at once upon the Plain:
Quick the next Burst succeeds, that scarce between
Short darting Intervals of Light are seen;
Till the whole Tempest spent, the Skies grow fair,
Smiling anew, and all serene the Air.

Then *Arskwin* started forth; and as he spoke,
Infernal Fury his whole Fabrick shook;
His blood-shot Eye-balls sparkl'd livid Flame,
And Sounds from his wide Mouth, scarce Human, came,

Dastards! he bawl'd; see your Destruction there;
By all the Gods, by this Right-Hand I swear!
Now shew the Prowess you so idly boast;
Or say, are all your doughty Heroes lost?
Are they from the first Charge already flown,
Or, like your God, invisible now grown?

Then DAVID forward sprung with ardent Zeal,
And thus reply'd, Behold, vile Infidel!
I send thee, Wretch, with thy own Eyes to prove,
If now thou seest him not, a God above!
Then with full Force, he the pois'd Jav'lin threw,
And certain of the Mark it whizzing flew:
Full in his gaping Mouth the Weapon sped,
And nail'd his venom'd Tongue up to his Head.
He falls, tho' stagg'ring first a while he stood,
And vomits out his Soul in Clots of Blood.

Alike in th' other Wing proud *Gurmund* far'd,
Who bold *Cadwgawn* to the Combat dar'd:
Advance, he cry'd, if yet thou fain wouldst know
The mighty Feats a *Gurmund*'s Arm can do!
No upstart Hero, high Descent I claim,
From Ancestors that fill the Rolls of Fame!

Why, (he return'd;) is all this Boasting shewn?
Vain Man, puff'd up with Honours not thy own!
Tread in their Steps; or call no longer thine
The Glories of the long illustrious Line:

Thy broken Faith, nor yet too late, renew;
Honour alone in Honour's Way purſue!

 Fool that thou art! the other ſtrait reply'd;
Honour takes as I pleaſe to either Side:
But hold, and hurling then his bearded Dart,
Here, Babler, take my Anſwer in thy Heart!
From his ſtrong Arm it ſhot along the Field,
The *Briton* ſoon receiv'd it on his Shield:
Nor ſtay'd, but back he ſent the ſwift Reply,
That harmleſs paſſing, glanc'd upon his Thigh.
To the cloſe Fight they then together came;
Their Courage equal, and their Strength the ſame.

 Like two four Bulls, that ruſhing on the Meads,
Aim furious for the Shock their curled Heads:
They ſtrike, they puſh, with claſhing Horns they gore,
And from hoarſe bloody Throats tremendous roar:
The while, at Gaze the Herds on either Hand,
Mute, panting for their Champion's Fortune, ſtand.

 With uneffectual Force the Warriors ſtrike,
Skilful to ward the coming Blows alike;
Long thus the dubious Combat they maintain'd,
Nor either loſt the Day, nor either gain'd;
Till *Gurmund* raging, heav'd a deadly Blow,
That meant at once to cleave the *Briton* thro';
He took the falling Thunder on his Shield,
But ſtun'd with the huge Force, he backward reel'd.

Yet

Yet soon again recov'ring to his Feet,
Hasted th' advancing Enemy to meet;
Full at his Head a noble Stroke he made,
And sprawling on the Ground th' *Hibernian* laid;
Then thro' his Bosom his bright Sword he bare,
And loos'd the Traytor's spotted Soul to Air.

The *Britons* see! nor more their Leaders know
To hold them in from Darting on the Foe.

As when a Torrent is by Dams withstood,
The crowding Waters swelling to a Flood,
Rush on at last, and with resistless Sway
Sweep Fences, Crops, and Villages away.

Strait with a gen'ral Shout they onward broke,
Nor could the *Saxons* stand the furious Shock:
O'erborn at once impetuous on their Rear,
Themselves upon their own Destruction bear.
Whole Ranks mow'd down together load the Plain,
And on, the *Britons* climb o'er Hills of Slain.
There, shorten'd of his Head, *Kanmera* dy'd,
A Mungril *Saxo-Pict*, and by his Side
Darvanter fell, their noblest Youth of all;
And worthy in a better Cause to fall!

No longer can they now sustain the Fight,
And *Fosta* howling led the scatter'd Flight:
With trilling Fear the ghastly Recreant shook,
And all around the swift Contagion took;

From one to one the Consternation seiz'd.
And each his own and Fellow's Fright encreas'd
They run, but fatally convinc'd, soon find
Their Fears and Foes not to be left behind
Not once to Face they turn 'em as they fly,
Or see the hostile Hand by which they die.
Along a dismal Havock mark'd the Road,
With Limbs, and LEEKS, and shatter'd Armour strew'd.
Eager Pursuit all Day the *Britons* made,
Till coming Night the bloody Labour stay'd:
Sounds the Retreat; when all their Colours seek,
And each his Helmet grac'd with *Saxon* LEEK.

 Enough, O *Britons!* then their DAVID said,
Sheath in the Scabbard now the weary Blade;
Return to needful Rest, repose away
The sore Fatigue of the laborious Day.
Sacred shall be to Morrow's Light, ordain'd
To solemn Joys, for Victory obtain'd
With LEEKS adorn'd we'll glad Processions go,
And pay to Heav'n the Debt of Thanks we owe:
Our Praise from Morn to Ev'ning shall ascend,
Nor with the Day, nor with our Lives shall end!
Then---But the pious Offices remain
To our brave Friends here for their Country slain,
Decent their dear Remains in Earth we'll lay,
And Tears and unavailing Honours pay:

O glorious Men! to Death you faithful stood,
And dy'd your Native Soil with noblest Blood;
Shed while it yet was warm in the just Cause
Of *True Religion, Liberty*, and *Laws!*

He spoke, their Approbation all declare,
And gladly to their sev'ral Tents repair.

'Twas now the dead still Season of the Night,
The Moon stole softly to Meridian Height;
The silent Stars all faint and languid show,
And all was hush'd and undisturb'd below:
The Chief, with the dull Weight of Sleep oppress'd,
Sunk down, and lay dissolv'd in balmy Rest.
In the soft Chains tho' fast the Senses bound,
Yet Fancy still proceeds its airy Round.
Ev'n then his *Britain*'s Fate employ'd his Thought,
And to his View this pleasing Vision brought.

A Virgin came, yet more than earthly Fair,
Tall was her Stature, and Divine her Air;
Loose her Attire, her Tresses unconfin'd
In Ringlets wav'd, and wanton'd in the Wind;
Her larger Eye-brows, with a manly Grace,
Enforc'd the milder Beauties of her Face.
By full-blown Charms, and chearful Aspect shown,
The Presence of gay LIBERTY was known!
With a bold Smile the bright celestial Maid,
The Chief, in daz'ling Glory lost, survey'd.

Then

Then from her lovely Mouth sweet Accents broke,
And thus in melting Melody she spoke.

  O Leader, favour'd with high *Heaven*'s Regard!
Her Patriot, how shall LIBERTY reward?
My *Britons* owe their Rights upheld to thee;
Long shalt thou live their happy Times to see;
With Blessings heap'd thy good old Age shall bend,
And to the Grave in perfect Peace descend!
Nor this enough to thee; whose publick Mind
Its Care extends to Ages yet behind,
Ev'n anxious for thy Country's future State!
Behold! I come her Fortunes to relate.

  Thus then: Almighty Wisdom has decreed,
Long with intestine Wars the *Isle* shall bleed:
Tho' all *Loegria* theirs the *Saxons* boast,
They'll find too hard to keep what *Britons* lost.
New Nations yet shall come, and these will feel
The Wrongs repay'd, they now to others deal:
Invasions shall their settl'd Rule annoy,
And still fresh Conquests shall the old destroy.

  Their wild Confusions, then a while, shall grant
The Respite which the harass'd *Britons* want:
Ah! could they civil Discord then refrain,
How might they win their ancient Realms again!
But oh! to their own Weal and Int'rest blind!
(As if they Ruin for themselves design'd)

Against their own, they impious Arms engage,
And *British* Victims fall to *British* Rage:
And thus self-conquer'd, they at last shall grow
A Prey too easy to the common Foe!
Yet not so far the Conquest shall obtain,
But still the Race shall unextinct remain:
Nor Time itself their Language e'er consume,
That, uncorrupted till the Day of Doom!

And now, O Saint! the better Prospect view,
See a long Course of golden Years renew!
Thro' the whole *Isle* the Jars at length shall cease,
The Nations all unite in endless Peace:
One Government, nor with unequal Rule,
From *Kernaw* shall extend to utmost *Thule*:
Nations distinct no more; but all the same,
And *Britain* the *One* universal Name!

Then HEAVEN itself the Monarchs shall ordain;
And chuse a Race o'er *Britons* fit to reign:
The bright Succession in a Prince shall rise,
Brave, Potent, Pious, Provident, and Wise!
Him, true Vicegerent of the King Supreme,
The Good shall honour, and the Bad blaspheme!
Not Brutes shall his just Laws of Reason bind,
But guard and govern Creatures of his Kind!

Then *Tyranny*, her Empire to regain,
Shall her last Efforts make, but make in vain:

From Men for ever exil'd she shall go,
With all her Plagues to rule her Hell below!

Nor must the ambient Sea his Pow'r confine,
New Provinces he shall to *Britain* joyn!
The *Saxon Elbe* shall swell her copious Tide,
With wealthy Freights her own rich Shores provide;
And *Thamisis* shall with the Burthen groan,
And make the foreign Product all his own.
Such his Decrees, who o'er the happy Lands
Shall gently then extend his mild Commands.
Glad Subjects shall be forward to obey,
And Peace and Plenty bless his Righteous Sway!

And when he to immortal Crowns above
Shall (late if Vows and Pray'rs avail!) remove;
His Regal Virtues deathless shall survive,
And in his SON, again the FATHER live!

HE, to perpetuate such a glorious Race,
Shall wed a PRINCESS of superior Grace:
And SHE, a *Cæsar's* Nuptials shall decline,
To be the Mother of this greater Line.
Roll on ye Years! around be swiftly hurl'd,
And give the promis'd Princess to the World!
Shed your best Influence then, ye Stars, on Earth!
And happy Omens tell th' auspicious Birth!

When the long Tract of Time shall finish'd be,
This Day, O Saint! th' auspicious Birth shall see:

This Day, that still its DAVID's Name shall bear,
And LEEKS adorn in each revolving Year!
Britons shall then be sooth'd from War's Alarms
To mutual Love, by her Celestial Charms.
Exhaustless Blessings from the Fair attend,
And see the Progeny from Heav'n descend!
But most the *Britons* of the Antient Line
Shall date new Joys from the propitious Sign:
This shall yet raise to Triumphs more sublime,
And mark *This Glorious Day* to the last End of Time!

FINIS.